"This is a good volume to get into the mood of Lent and it is especially helpful on those days the church commemorates the passion and death of Our Lord."

Msgr. Charles Diviney
The Brooklyn Tablet

"John D. Powers has made each of the ten witnesses flawed humans who had just a rudimentary understanding of what was going on around them that day. Each witness portrayed here is good material for meditation and discussion, and would make an effective teaching tool."

Intermountain Catholic

"...the ten witnesses of the passion of Jesus tell not only what the passion meant to them, but what it means for people now. The cross maker, for example, begs 20th-century readers to 'watch closely as Christ carries his cross today and ask yourself if, by your silent indifference, you have helped to carve that cross.'"

North Texas Catholic

"Father Powers shares in dramatic monologues what his heart heard and his imagination perceived as he read about ten witnesses of the passion of Jesus."

Catholic Twin Circle

"There is something mischievous about sidling up to those less than saintly persons in the Bible to find out what they are thinking....Fr. Powers allows us to do this with the sleeping disciple James, the despairing Judas, the mocking soldier, along with Mary the Mother and John the Beloved. We walk away from this book seeing the saints more human and the sinners more saintly than we ever gave them credit for."

Carroll Stuhlmueller, C.P.
Catholic Theological Union

"In a different approach to lenten reading, *If They Could Speak* relates to ten witnesses of the passion of Jesus. They each offer their story on how the crucifixion changed their lives and how that event should change the life of every Christian.... "

The Catholic Observer

"In an impressive book, Fr. Powers has 10 witnesses to the passion of Jesus tell us their intimate thoughts—personal responses that will release each reader's own reaction."

Prairie Messenger

"What were the thoughts of those directly involved in the crucifixion of Jesus? Father Powers uses his considerable imaginative skill to reflect on ten witnesses of Christ's passion. They give a sense of 'being there.'"

Spiritual Book News

JOHN D. POWERS

If They Could Speak

Ten Witnesses to the Passion of Jesus

To Lorraine,

Peace in the Passion,

Fr. John Powers S.

XXIII
TWENTY-THIRD PUBLICATIONS
Mystic, Connecticut

All Scripture passages are taken from
The New Jerusalem Bible,
Readers Edition, Garden City, N.Y., Doubleday, 1966

Illustrations by Judy Brauch

Fifth printing 1997

Twenty-Third Publications
185 Willow Street
P.O. Box 180
Mystic, CT 06355
(860) 536-2611
800-321-0411

ISBN 0-89622-421-x
Library of Congress Catalog Card No. 89-51902

Contents

Dedication

This book of imaginings
flows from my commited relationship
to a community of Brothers, Sisters, Lay Associates, and Priests
dedicated to promote, in deed and word, a hope-filled devotion
to the message of love proclaimed by the Cross of Christ:

THE PASSIONIST COMMUNITY

Introduction

*W*hen you read the Bible, do you hear voices? I do. I am not talking about voices that create sound waves for the ear to hear; rather I speak of a divinely creative voice that eternally speaks to the human heart through Scripture.

If you truly desire to hear the voice of God through the Hebrew and Christian Scriptures, there is something more you must open than just the cover of this book. You must first open your miraculously inventive and all-too-frail human imagination. As Franz Rosenzweig, the inspired and inspiring scholar, the agnostic transformed by Christ, the Jewish sage of Frankfurt in the early 1890s, has said:

> The Bible is different from all other books. You can know what is in other books only by reading them. But there are two ways of knowing what is in the Bible: first, by listening to what the Bible says; second, by listening to the beating of the human heart....The Bible and the heart say the same thing (*Western Spirituality*, Fides/Claretian, 1979, p. 405).

In its every passage, the Bible beats with the spirit-filled power of a supremely imaginative God. As the foundation of all reality, God is revealed through all that is, especially through human beings. God is the "imagineer"; we are God's

1

image. Flowing from the divine image-maker is the human imagination, created to lead the way to the source of all reality.

To a large extent, of course, what we discover or hear when reading the Hebrew and Christian Scriptures depends upon what we bring to the reading in the first place: an open or hardened heart, a desire for inspiration or a demand for specific answers, a faith-filled imagination or a predetermined interpretation.

Through the envisioning power of the mind and heart we can know and experience the reality of God beyond mere logical analysis. If we listen in attentive faith to our own God-given, intuitive and inventive imaginations, especially as we read and hear the Sacred Scriptures, we can hear the many challenging, gentle, protesting and pleading voices from the Bible. These voices speak with a strength great enough to change the world, or at least to transform radically our little worlds.

What I have attempted to do in this brief book of active meditations is to share some of what my heart has heard and my imagination has perceived as I read stories from Scripture. I have attempted to give voice to some familiar and some not-so-familiar characters from the Bible, people who participated in some dramatic way in the life, suffering, and death of Jesus Christ.

I hope you will find as much drama, excitement, and inspiration in reading these meditations as I did in writing them (and so often do in performing them). As you slowly read these meditations, I hope the purpose of this book will be achieved in some small way: that your hearts and imaginations might be opened to the one voice of God that speaks *to you* through the many voices in Scripture.

One last thought before you turn to the first Bible voice. As you know, listening is an art that demands patience and calm. *When* you choose to read these monologue meditations (whether one a day, one a week, or all in one sitting) is not as important as *how* you read—and listen—to them. If you approach this simple book with an unhurried heart, you will hear more through your own spirit-filled imagination than you ever thought possible.

James, the Sleeping Disciple

When Jesus returned to his disciples, he found them asleep. He said to Peter, "So you could not stay awake with me for even an hour? Be on guard and pray that you may not undergo the test. The spirit is willing but nature is weak...." Once more, on his return, he found them asleep; they could not keep their eyes open. Jesus left them again, withdrew somewhat, and began to pray a third time, saying the same words as before. Finally, he returned to his disciples and said to them: "Sleep on now. Enjoy your rest! The hour is on us when the Son of Man is to be handed over to the power of evil men. Get up! Let us be on our way! See, my betrayer is here." *(Matthew 26:40, 41, 43, 46)*

I, James, come to you, friends, with head bowed in shame, for I am one of the followers of Christ who lay sleeping in the Garden of Gethsemane while he wept in torment and prayer. I could give you many excuses why I failed to be present to my brother Jesus during his most painful time of agony. I could tell you that I was just exhausted from the many miles we had recently traveled; fatigued from the overwhelming excitement of our grand entrance into Jerusalem only days before. But to be honest with you—and that is why I am here—there is no excuse. There is no defense, valid or otherwise, that can justify my uncaring attitude toward the one man who cared for me beyond all human expectations.

I was a respected follower of Jesus. I traveled with him throughout Israel, healing, teaching, and preaching, and with great success, I might add. The crowds grew larger wherever we traveled. Every day more and more needy people reached out to the Lord for healing. Wherever Jesus went, he was a success. Because I walked with him, as one of his chosen, I was treated with the same respect. I must confess that I liked the adulation, the admiration of the crowds. It filled me with enthusiasm, and, yes, I admit it, self-importance.

I was envied by the multitudes at the gates of Jerusalem, and loved by those whom Jesus healed of physical and emotional pain. Christ's success was my success. When I heard my name spoken with respect in the same sentence as the name of my master, I felt a sense of pride that was difficult to control. It was so very good to walk with Jesus during the good times.

With my self-inflated attitude, however, I began to grow lazy, taking for granted the full mission of the Lord of Life. As his admirers began to dwindle, fearing rumors that the Roman soldiers had orders to arrest Jesus and his companions, my heart began to cower, and my excitement turned to confusion. My eyes began to close with daydreams and fantasies of the days when my enthusiasm helped me to deal with the more difficult demands of Christ's teaching of love beyond measure.

As Jesus wept in the garden of his most personal pain, anguishing before the face of death, my eyes were covered with darkness, so that I could not see the necessary sacrifices demanded of one called to love as Jesus loved. I didn't sleep in the garden because I was tired. I slept because I was afraid, terrified of an uncertain but surely dangerous future. Where was all the adulation? Where was all the wondrous excitement?

Even when my beloved friend, Jesus, shook me awake and shared his terror, I did not listen, but rather turned over to hide in fear. My mind, body, and heart were controlled by the same terror that Jesus faced, yet I could not wake. If I could not face my own anguish, how could I possibly face his?

What a fool I was to ignore the one person who had so many times transformed my life with his love! No one had ever blessed me so much, yet I ignored his hour of greatest need. When I needed Jesus he was there, but when his need rose up I lay sleeping.

I, James, come to you today on behalf of my fellow fearful disciples, Peter and John, to shake you from your sleepy avoidance of reality. It took me years to learn that if you choose to travel the way of Jesus you must face your deepest fears, confront your most demonic insecurities and stand firm before the great desire to always travel the way of comfort, pleasure, and self-importance.

Awake and see that Jesus needs you today to bravely continue his work of love! Do not grow lazy with comfort and success, and think there is nothing to be done. Do not let the fear of failure prevent you from hearing Christ when he calls you through the voices of those in need. Jesus needs you today as much as he needed me on that dreadful night in the garden. He needs you to wake up from your fearful and fitful sleep to help those who suffer most to face the future with hope. You are Christ's light of courage shining in the world today, and even the dullest light can dispel darkness.

Open your eyes, my friends, to the agony that is suffered in your garden as your brothers and sisters face a future of continued poverty, illness, loneliness, and oppression. Wake up to the agony of Christ on your streets, in your homes and hospitals, in your prisons and unemployment lines, in the young and elderly. Do not take the Lord's mission for granted and think that it is someone else's task to care courageously for others. Right now the lord of the garden calls you to help him do what must be done if hope is to prosper and grow.

The test of real discipleship is before you now, as it was before me in the garden so many years ago. Do not be content to hide in fear or sleepy comfort, for the Lord will continue to challenge you to respond in faith. If you work to love as you have been loved, with eyes open to the cruel agony that rages in the world today, with hands, hearts, and spirits ready, you can defeat the enemy of apathy and pass the test of compassion.

Prayer

Lord Jesus, as the disciples slept in the garden of your greatest agony, ignoring your deepest needs, so I am often blind to the needs of those who suffer today. With tricks of mind and heart I can so easily rationalize my laziness and lack of care, sleeping my life away with temporary distractions and petty concerns.

My blindness pushes the needs of others to the bottom of my priority list, while my own comfort rests securely at the top of my concerns. Wake me, Lord Jesus, from my drowsiness so that I may hear you cry out with pain in the voices of my suffering brothers and sisters.

Help me overcome my fear of what others may think and say of me if I serve as you served, bless as you blessed, and love those most in need, as you so compassionately continue to love me. Amen.

The Despairing Judas

Then Judas, who had handed Jesus over, seeing that Jesus had been condemned, began to regret his action deeply. He took the thirty pieces of silver back to the chief priests and elders and said, "I did wrong to deliver up an innocent man!" They retorted, "What is that to us? It is your affair!" So Judas flung the money into the temple and left. He went off and hanged himself. (*Matthew 27:3-5*)

I am Judas, perhaps better known to you as the accomplice of evil, a son of perdition, a traitor and conspirator. Whatever you may call me, out of anger, know this. I just did not understand. I was blinded by my greed, fear, and need for acceptance and power. I thought I understood what Jesus was about, that his mission was to take full control and authority from the Romans and Council of Elders; but I was so terribly wrong. So stupidly wrong. In my greed, the evil one rose up and said, "Take what you can." In my need, he proclaimed, "This Jesus loves the others but not you." I was in awe of Jesus but hungered for his acceptance. I wanted to be important in his eyes.

I know, I know. Don't look at me as you do. There is no rationale that can justify my treacherous actions. I am quite aware that I committed one of the greatest sins in history: I betrayed a friend unto death. I have lived with the regret for what seems an eternity.

The reason I come to you today is to tell you that yes, it is true, I have been guilty of betrayal—but I have also been forgiven by the very love I conspired against. I know it sounds unbelievable, but it is true. Christ forgave me by his very death. It was I who could not forgive myself.

It has taken me generations upon generations of eternal living to realize that I have been forgiven, even for my most treacherous sin. Today I stand before you and God, healed and reconciled, washed clean and forgiven. How do I know this to be true, you wonder? It was the kiss in the garden.

When I so crudely stepped up to Jesus to embrace him with a sign that marked his identity, he revealed who he truly was: the long-awaited Messiah. When I kissed the master, I honestly expected that he would call upon all the magical powers of Yahweh to protect him from the Roman soldiers. I fully expected Jesus to confront the soldiers with his miraculous gifts. Such a display would have convinced his would-be attackers of his true identity, and that joining him in opposition to the Romans and Sanhedrin was the only logical course of action.

It was not until I kissed the Lord that I realized that he would never use power to overcome the minds and hearts of others. When I looked into his eyes, I knew that I had been so grievously wrong. I realized I knew nothing of the man, even after all our travels together. When he allowed me to kiss him and returned my kiss with an embrace, I knew that he indeed loved me as one of his own. He loved me enough to understand why I had betrayed him, and to forgive me without my asking him to.

As the soldiers finally led Jesus away, I was stunned by the awareness that my desire to help him rule by strength was itself a lie, motivated not by selfless concern, but rather, steeped in my need and greed. It was not domination that Jesus sought but simply love, a powerful force that could set people free to choose life.

I was a blind and deluded man who turned against the very person who could convince me that I was worth something in the eyes of God. I hated myself enough to help kill the one who could save me from my self-destructive ways. What I wanted—control, success and power—I did not get. What I desperately needed—the love of another—I received a hundredfold in the friendship and forgiveness of Christ. It took my treason and his death, however, to prove this to me.

As I despaired in my sinfulness, despising myself enough to seek death, the grace of Christ befriended me. You may think me arrogant, but truly, my friends, I know the Lord is now with me. I shall never say that my self-deception was anything but evil. I shall always hate what I have done. I know, however, that the Lord has set me free from my sin and self-hate for eternal living.

I do not share myself with you today, however, to seek your forgiveness, to convince you that I was justified in my actions, or even to beg for your understanding. How you feel about me is unimportant. No, I come to you today, my friends, to convince you that as I was released from the prison of despair and self-destruction, so can you. As the Lord of all life has forgiven me, the greatest of sinners, so he loves you enough to do the same.

Fearful one, I know that you may have sinned against Christ, perhaps by turning your back on those in need and refusing to walk as his follower. I know that you may have kissed the Lord with false and shallow religious sentiment, motivated by the desire for a comfortable faith, only to turn away as he was being crucified on your streets and in your wars.

My sinning friends, I have been the most frightened of the Lord's chosen. I felt so helpless and hungry for love that I was no longer able to see love when it stood right before me. My friends, allow your sins to be forgiven, open your sealed hearts and accept the acceptance of Christ. Let the grace of the Lord befriend you today, so that you may walk as a conspirator of love in a world that hungers for forgiveness.

Prayer

Lord Jesus, as you walked to your cross of pain, Judas hid in the shadows of his guilt and shame, despairing of your love. Yet, despite his betrayal, you, Lord, forgave him with your very death and resurrection.

Help me understand and accept that you love me with the same uncompromising love, that even when I turn from you with a mocking kiss of sin, you continue to bless me with your covenant promise.

When I sell you, Lord, for the silver of greed or the coins of power, fear, and pain, drown me in your friendship.

When I sin, my eternal companion, embrace me with the arms of your forgiveness. Amen.

Pilate

Pilate said to the crowd, "Then what am I to do with Jesus, the so-called Messiah?" "Crucify him!" they all cried. He said, "Why, what crime has he committed?" But they only shouted louder, "Crucify him!" Pilate finally realized that he was making no impression and that a riot was breaking out. He called for water and washed his hands in front of the crowd, declaring as he did so, "I am innocent of the blood of this man. The responsibility is yours." (*Matthew 27:22-24*)

The truth was simply not a commodity that I dealt with. I did not know who this Jesus really was, and I certainly did not care that the crowd screamed for his blood. Their self-complacent and self-righteous piety was merely threatened by a man of some wisdom and, as far as I was concerned, innocent of insurrection.

I was just a politician, a procurator under the emperor Tiberius. I dealt only with whatever compromising convenience would keep the people quiet, content, and under control. I never thought that I would ever admit it in public, but I was also a coward.

What could I do? The angry mob brought this Jesus to me, determined to have him crucified. They had no concern for justice or rights of any kind. I had no choice. Either I let this guiltless Jesus be led away to death to please the crowd or I set him free, only to pay with my position of authority. The mob would have nothing of mercy, even on their holy day. I admit I did try to convince the crowd, perhaps without much conviction, that this Jesus seemed to be an innocent man. But their hatred would not relent. It was I who finally yielded, giving Jesus up to their arrogance and fear.

Ultimately, however, I proved to be just as cruel as those who screamed for Jesus's death, for I had the authority to decide his fate. I learned long ago that you should not fear your enemies, for they can only kill you. Nor should you be frightened of your friends, for they can only reject you. The people you must always be cautious of are those who do not care, for it is the callous who allow the killers and traitors to ply their trade.

I know I share in the responsibility for Jesus' sentence of death, for I was just cowardly enough to be indifferent. I chose to wash my hands of any and all concern for his blood. I decided not to make a decision, but to let the crowd have its way. Thus, I participated in his death as surely as if I'd nailed him to the cross myself. What a fool I was to think that I could simply clean my hands of my obligation to the truth.

Don't turn away, now, as though you are astonished by my cowardice. You see this sort of thing every day, when politicians place their own gain over the interests of those in need. You hear them saying still, "Well, I only followed orders," when those in authority think themselves infallible. When your laws are perverted by corruption, your preachers bend the truth to please you, or your institutions tell you what not to read or think, then I, Pilate, live again in you, washing my hands of the sentence being so unjustly passed on the innocent of today.

I live within you when you kneel in your stained glass churches, yet ignore the pleas of the oppressed, the poor, the forgotten and sick. It is the Pilate in you who proclaims, "It is not my responsibility if the rich get richer and the poor get poorer. What can I do, after all? I am only one person." I am the compromiser in you who wants only to avoid the difficult decisions, to ignore the rights of others, and to sit on the fence of every moral issue. I am the one who justifies cruelty in the name of self-defense, brutality for the sake of power. I am the one in you who turns away when you are called to stand firm for the truth.

If there was one thing I saw in this Jesus as he so silently stood before me in the emperor's court, it was that there can be no freedom for those who compromise or bargain with the truth. However, this Jesus you so profess to love no longer stands before me for judgment. I have made my mistake and am paying the price for cowardice. This same

Christ, however, does stand directly before you today, in the desperate needs of those afflicted by emotional, physical, and social oppression. Christ is in your homes and on your streets, challenging you to care enough to set him free.

How often have you, Christian, like me, washed your hands with pious platitudes and rejected Jesus with a shallow religiosity that makes no noise and moves no mountain of injustice? Your neighbor suffers and, like me, you so often relinquish your power to help alleviate that suffering for fear of what others will think. Today, look within yourself for the Pilate that trembles in cowardice. I am the part of you that is robed in sentimental piety or rationalized ignorance. I am that part of you that shakes with fear in the face of challenging truth and demanding love.

Man or woman of faith, do not allow your fear to rule your ability to make tough decisions, to judge justly, and to act wisely. Do not wash the truth away with the need to please or the desire for power, as I did. Instead, my friends, let the silent courage of Jesus stand with you as you speak your truth with love, no matter what the cost.

Prayer

Lord Jesus, liberate me from my fears of what others may think of me because I believe. Grant me the courage to see the truth of your love and hold on to it, to speak the truth of your wisdom without perverting it, and to share the truth of your hope without compromise.

Set me free from my desire to take the easy way, to avoid my obligation to defend the oppressed, the victimized, and the mistreated. Never let me wash my hands of responsibility as others clamor for vindictive violence.

Teach me, Lord, that "certain rights are acquired by

a human being just in the act of being born:

The right to grow and meet one's individual potentialities.

The right to appraise and apply's one's abilities, consistent with the rights of others.

The right to one's thoughts—the right to nourish them and voice them.

The right to make mistakes, whether of thought or deed, without fear of unjust punishment.

The right to hope.

The right to justice, whether the claim is against a person, the masses, or government itself.

The right to contemplate human destiny and the mysteries of existence, or to detach oneself altogether from these pursuits.

The right to hold grievances against one's society and to make them known to others

The right to make a better life for our young." Amen.*

*Human Options by Norman Cousins (New York: Berkley Books), 1983, p. 63.

The Crossmaker

The whole people said in reply, "Let Jesus' blood be on us and our children." At this Pilate released Barabbas to them. Jesus, however, he first had scourged; then he handed him over to be crucified. (*Matthew 27:25-26*)

My name is not important. All you need know is that I am a crossmaker. Along with many other carpenters in the city of Jerusalem, I was pressed into the service of carving the crossbeams used for crucifixion by the brutish Romans. What could I do? I had to feed my family. Although I knew full well how the Romans used these beams, I could do nothing to prevent it.

Each morning I would go to the hills to cut down strong pieces of timber and drag them home for carving. Once chiseled, they were piled high in the Romans' courtyard. It was not a task I cherished, but the money put food on the table. Mine was a poor family and it was my duty to take care of them. How these crossbeams were used was not my responsibility, not mine to question. My first responsibility was to my wife and children.

Oh, when I think back on the days of my apprenticeship, when I first took up the trade of a carpenter, I can recall the joy I felt when carving a table from coarse pieces of heavy wood. I have always thought myself a skilled carpenter. Not the best, perhaps, but one in love with the craft. It is an art, you know, to mold and fashion from rough beams a smooth and well-fitted piece of furniture. It takes an eye of care and hands of compassion. This may sound strange to those of you who do not know the feel of wood, but to be a true carpenter you must respect the grain and bend of each and every beam you cut or it will not fit well.

I sound like a dreamer, and I was, so many years ago. Then reality hit me with the cruelty of a world gone mad. My ideals seemed to fall away like the bark of a dying tree. With each problem and setback, I became more and more pessimistic and uncaring. Even the love of my craft seemed to slowly crack into splinters of callous indifference. My art became a tool of death, my craft a means of suffering, and I did not seem to care. My friends, it is one thing to say, "I did not know," when finding fault with your actions. It is another thing entirely to know your actions contribute to the heavy burdens placed on the shoulders of another and to say, "I don't care." Not knowing is ignorance and can be understood; not caring is the very evil Christ came to overcome.

You may wonder why I have come to speak with you today. I, Christ's crossmaker, watched this holy man carry upon his shoulders what I had chiseled with indifference and hewed with arrogance, and I became sick with shame. I beg you, my friends, to watch the suffering Jesus of today's crucifixion walk the steps of passion as innocent children go hungry, family violence increases, and the helpless are mired in mindless bureaucracy. Watch Jesus nailed to the cross of today's violence as the powerless are victimized by weapons of a holocaust, built out of fear.

Watch closely as Christ carries his cross today and ask yourself if, by your silent indifference, you have helped to carve that cross. If so, put down you hammer of abuse, your blade of debasement, for I guarantee you, no one carves a cross for another to shoulder without one day having to carry it himself.

Prayer

Lord Jesus, for how many ages have you remained imprisoned upon your cross, and still I pass you by, ignoring you? How often have I overlooked your tender presence in my life, paying little attention to your great sorrow, your pain, your powerful love? How often have I, by indifference, added to you sorrow, deepened your pain, and refused your love?

You constantly stretch forth your hands to re-create me, to touch me with your love, and still I close my eyes to your presence and force you to remain imprisoned upon your cross. Yet my name is written in your heart forever, and you will not allow me to ignore you or run from you. You have loved me with an everlasting love, and I continue to place obstacles in your path.

Your cross shows me, however, the power of your love, that it is stronger than my fear, that it can overcome my need to run from you. Lord, let the love that flows from your cross surround me, break down the walls of my fear, and fill my heart.

Lord Jesus Christ crucified, teach us how to love one another, as you have loved us, even to the cross. Amen.

The Mocking Soldier

The procurator's soldiers took Jesus inside the praetorium and collected the whole cohort around him. They stripped off his clothes and wrapped him in a scarlet military cloak. Weaving a crown out of thorns, they fixed it on his head, and stuck a reed in his right hand. Then they began to mock him by dropping to their knees before him saying, "All hail, King of the Jews!" They also spat on him. Afterward they took hold of the reed and kept striking him on the head. (*Matthew 27:27-30*)

There is one thing I know how to do, one talent I have developed over the years as captain of the procurator's cohort of soldiers, and that was the art of abuse. I could direct my soldiers to use just the right combination of physical and verbal violence so that any man, no matter how strong, would crumble to his knees with a stunning swiftness.

I am not quite sure why I was invited to speak today, though. All I did was my job and duty. When ordered to flog and humiliate a sentenced man, I would simply assign the task to a few of my loyal soldiers and stand back to watch as the task was handled with care and effectiveness. As guards of the procurator's court, we had little else to occupy our time but the diversion of flogging someone now and then. I had led such beatings a hundred times before this self-proclaimed prophet of yours, this Jesus, appeared before me.

At the time, Jesus was just a common and lowly Galilean. He meant nothing to me. The only reason I would have remembered him at all (if he did not profoundly change my life) was that he was the only Galilean I ever met who claimed to be a king. We thought most of his class to be rather simple-minded at best. But, if it was king he wanted to be, so be it, I thought. I made him the king of criminals as I inflicted on him every cruel trick I could think of. I was determined to show this low-class Jesus that no one mocks Roman authority with foolish claims of divinity.

My task was to humble him with disdain, strip and beat him, pure and simple. I even came up with the idea of fashioning a crown of thorns for the new king to wear with majesty and glory. I was to teach him and his followers that no one could stand against the power of the Romans and win. A few mocking touches to humiliate him were just what I needed to get the message across.

Yet, with all the bloody scorn, vile ridicule and arrogant sarcasm, I could not strip this supposed holy man of his dignity. Despite the brutal flogging and bloody crown, I could not break the spirit of this Jesus. In my cruel attempt to humble this Christ, it was I who was brought to my knees in humiliation.

I instructed my soldiers to use every vicious technique I knew, yet this man of Galilee stood in brazen silence. As I watched, I wanted to scream at him, "For your so-called God's sake, cry out, you fool. Don't hold your pain in silence, for it will only make matters worse. Scream and screech again, beg and whimper and we will stop this torture!" No one had ever stood the whipping with silence before and it drove me and my soldiers mad with anger.

As I continued to watch the soldiers fail in their efforts to bend and break this man of infuriating silence, my anger began to change. As I stared for a moment at the crown that had been pushed down over his head, I suddenly realized that beating in the bloody breast of the man who stood strong before me was not the heart of an evil or insane man. From years of experience, I knew what the heart of the most vicious criminal was like. With his silent courage, this man Jesus forced me to gaze into my own heart, and I was appalled at what I found there.

The strength of this man's passionate beliefs was so great that even I began to wonder if he could be more than I first judged. It was the silence that ultimately ate into what little conscience I had left and convinced me that he had to be a holy, sacred figure, one gifted with something divine, one to be listened to, not silenced by tyranny and abuse.

Just as I was so arrogant and ignorant as to mock the son of God so many years ago, there are those in your time who scorn Jesus with brutal bigotry. How many of your neighbors are oppressed with ridicule because of the color of their skin or the creed of their faith? How many are beaten and bloodied by hungry power-seekers whose hearts have been frozen by years of comfort and control?

You do not have to go back in time to imagine what Christ's crucifixion was like. I was there and can testify to its ugliness. In fact, I helped to make it so. No, do not wish that you were there. There is plenty of crucifixion to go around today without having to return to Christ's historical agony.

If you are a person with any faith, you must then realize that it is your very faith, weak as it may be, that makes the Jesus I flogged your contemporary. He lives, suffers, dies, and rises today, right in your midst, as surely as he did in my time.

I may have actually been there, participating in the crucifixion of Jesus, but I confess to you I understood very little even when my eyes were opened to who it was who suffered before me. You are here today, my friends, at Christ's crucifixion in your own world. Are you involved in flogging Christ? Does contemporary suffering confront your conscience the way Jesus' torture confronted mine? When your kin in the human family are ridiculed or mocked, does it break your heart and fill you with just rage? When others—people of a different race or color, homeless people, gays and lesbians—are disdained, do you close your eyes with indifference or open them with the awareness that Jesus shares in their suffering? When your neighbors are crowned with the thorns of bigotry, do you see in them the pain of Jesus?

Listen, Christian, to the silence that hides the pain of this world, the cries for justice and the pleas for equality and fall to your knees. Pray that you will not be one of the horde that mocks Christ today by flogging him with preconceived, dogmatic and self-righteous judgments. Remember, Christian, every judgment you pass on another you pass on yourself.

Prayer

Lord of silent dignity, breathe in me a passionate spirit that fills my heart with justice for all your kin.

Lord of patient purpose, kindle in me a fervent flame that burns brightly against the darkness of tyranny.

Lord of hushed courage, inspire in me a swelling confidence to speak out against savage inhumanity.

Lord of stillness, encourage in me a furious love that builds peace in the human family.

Lord of today, teach me to see your suffering in my own home, neighborhood, workplace, and society and to care enough not only to stop adding to the pain but to let my heart be forever changed by your compassion. Amen.

A Woman of Jerusalem

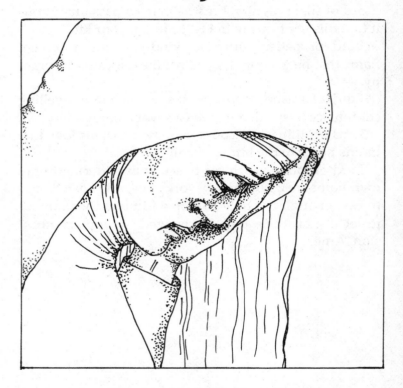

A great crowd of people followed Jesus, including women who beat their breasts and lamented over him. Jesus turned to them and said: "Daughters of Jerusalem, do not weep for me. Weep for yourselves and for your children." (*Luke 23:27-28*)

Jesus, I cry for the children, because their future seems blinded by our darkness. I weep often for the little ones who will need so much protection in the dark. Who is it though, Lord, who will weep for you? Who is it but those who so desperately need your strength and hope?

You must have felt so terribly alone as you stumbled along the path of your crucifixion, and all I could do was stand there and cry. As your heart was broken with rejection and abandonment, my heart mourned for those who did not believe in your passionate love. How much they missed by ignoring you as you passed by, Lord!

As I watched you carry that ugly beam of wood, falling often from its burdensome weight, I wanted to shriek in anger at the cruelty of those unbelievers who did this to you. "Why have you done this to the one person who could have filled your dark lives with some bright meaning?" This was the most important man ever to walk among us, and we allowed his flame to be snuffed out because it cast threatening shadows over our fearful hearts. What cowards the men of Rome and of the Sanhedrin are. Every tear that fell from my eyes was a silent and angry protest, "How can you be so blind that you would kill the one who can save, crucify the one who could liberate?" As Jesus walked his path of passion, I followed only footsteps behind, grieving for the world's loss.

I know that there were many in the crowd, pressed against the buildings to clear a path, who thought my tearful mourning was a foolish spectacle and I was a naive woman who just did not understand what was politically necessary. I may not be the wisest of women, but I do know one thing. If the only place politically inclined men can lead us is into more of the same darkness, exchanging war for progress, and increased brutality for advancement, then let us find and follow a new leader. Let us follow the one who came to give us a simpler way, a way out of the shadows.

Jesus proved he was not just another politician who bargained away his values by doing the one thing a "party" man would never do: die for love. Jesus died for the life of the little ones and for the future, that it may be forever young and hopeful. I may have made an emotional scene as I mourned the Lord's passing but at least I saw him for who he was. Others looked for God only after the Lord had passed. I was determined not to lose sight of the life-giving light, even if it took me to the cross.

When Jesus noticed me and the other neighborhood women crying in helplessness, he paused in our direction to speak. Another person would have protested his innocence or made his needs known, but Jesus did not concern himself with his pain, his sorrow. This Jesus died as he lived, caring for those who could not care for themselves. He wept for others as he himself faced death. Could there ever be a brighter, more hope-giving light than this son of God? With a few simple words, Jesus turned my grieving heart and confused mind from him to all the innocent of the land. His words gave me a way, a purpose, a love I could share.

It was not until days later, when I was preparing a meal, that the lesson Jesus taught me reminded me of a story from my childhood. It was the story of a man who was famous throughout the land for his writings. He had written scroll upon scroll of brilliant musings and had shared them throughout the kingdom with the less learned. When he died he was lifted up into the heavens of judgment, where he saw many people in a long line. They must be awaiting their last reward, he thought, so he went to take his place in line, carrying with him all the scrolls he had penned during his life. He was heavily weighted with his writings on philosophy and law, business and money-changing. As he took his place in line, he noticed standing in front of him was a small and frail woman of many years. She looked poor and uneducated, so it surprised the scholar greatly to see that she, too, was carrying a scroll. Curiosity got the best of him, so finally he asked the old woman, "Tell me, please, what kind of writing does your scroll contain?" With surprise in her eyes, the frail old woman looked at the heavily burdened man and said simply, "Why, this is the scroll upon which is written the names of all the children I have loved. I was informed that I had to bring it with me in order to go through into eternity." The man then realized that he had brought the wrong scrolls.

My friends, what Jesus taught me that agonizing day on the streets of Jerusalem is that in every child's pain he is suffering in innocence. Jesus taught me that in every mother's hurt, he is bruised, and in every act of injustice, he is forced to take another step on his passion journey. I learned that fateful day to feed the hungry children, for if you do not feed them you kill them. The reason I cried, and still do in prayer, is because I loved this Jesus of Nazareth. Losing him seemed much too much to bear. He, however, taught me to transform the very energy of my mourning into a purposeful love for those still in darkness.

When even a small portion of justice dies, we all must cry. When a single act of care is held back, we should all mourn the loss, and when the slightest part of peace is renounced with violence, we must all shed a tear in grief for the world has been rendered a bit less human. We must then, however, let our grief turn to passion-filled rage so that we can begin again to care. In this way, Jesus will never die. He will be remembered always in the names of those children whom we love.

Prayer

Where there is pain, God is present.
Where there is despair, hope is hidden.
Where there is oppression, freedom will rise.

Where there is hurt, healing waits.
Where there is conflict, peace shall again be born.
Where there is death, new life can grow.

If only we have eyes that can see in the dark. Amen.

Simon, the Cyrenean

As the soldiers led Jesus away, they laid hold of one Simon the Cyrenean, who was coming in from the fields. They put a crossbeam on Simon's shoulder for him to carry along behind Jesus. (*Luke 23:26*)

Let me tell you right from the start: I was there when this Jesus was being led to crucifixion. I saw the entire affair and it was brutal. I never planned on being there on the city streets nor did I want any involvement in the matter. It was entirely by chance that I became entangled in the mess. My wife had become something of a devotee of this Nazarene but I avoided any concern for the man, until the day I ended up unwillingly carrying his crossbeam.

The day I was thrust into the middle of the Lord's suffering had begun like any other. My companions and I had been working in the fields, harvesting a very prosperous crop, when we were told that we could leave work early because of the sabbath. None of us was going to question the landowner's pious religious customs so we took advantage of the opportunity and on the way home stopped for a few mugs of wine. Making our way home, at the end of a hard day's work, was always a joyful time, a time for trading stories, telling tales and laughing without control, usually all the way to the city gates where we had to go our separate ways.

As I passed through the city—on the day Jesus confronted me with a most demanding question—I noticed the crowds waiting for what had to be another victim of crucifixion. This was the only event that could bring out such a crowd, along with the merchants, pickpockets, and dignitaries. I did the best I could to skirt the cruel scene, when I overheard someone say that it was the prophet, Jesus, who would soon turn the corner on his way to Golgotha. With that information, I decided to pause for a moment to get a look at this man my wife had spoken so often about. The least I could do would be to fill her in on the spectacle of the day.

I'm not quite sure if reporting to my wife was the only reason I stopped to stare at the crucifixion. I suppose it was also the fact that I had never seen a self-proclaimed king led off to the slaughter before and, of course, we humans do tend to have a rather morbid curiosity when it comes to someone else's pain.

It was in the midst of the chaos, as Jesus was passing right in front of where I stood, that I suddenly found myself looking at the point of a sword's blade thrust directly in front of my face. "You there," someone said as though from a great distance, "get over here and carry that beam. We don't want the king to die before we get him to his throne." Arms grabbed at me, pulled me forward, pushed me down and laid at least a 10-stone weight of coarse wood on my back.

I was shaking and scared as I realized that I had been forced to involve myself with a convicted criminal. I became frightened when the thought struck me that perhaps the soldiers picked me for this task because they thought I was a follower of this man. I protested angrily but was told to shut up and do what I was told. I did exactly that, hoping my silence would demonstrate that I was not associated with this criminal.

Then, something happened that would change the course of my life as dramatically as the soldiers had changed my customary route home. As I leaned down to heave the beam higher on my shoulders, I looked straight into the face of Jesus. He looked exhausted and was covered with blood, yet in his eyes was the fire of his purpose. Physically near collapse, his eyes were yet filled with the strength of a faith so strong that I knew this man was like no other. His eyes finally met mine and as they did they took hold of my spirit, filling my heart with words that will echo there forever. Despite the fact that by my help I quickened the Lord's end, I continue to hear him say to me what he said that day, "My brother, talk to me of your faith."

"My faith?" I responded, aloud. "What faith are you talking about?" I asked, so all could hear me challenge him. "I don't even know you," I said somewhat callously as I turned away to the task of carrying his cross. It was then that he stumbled and as I reached over to steady his steps he said again, "Talk to me of your faith, my friend."

The question finally hit its mark and I began to think as we continued the journey up the steep stone steps of the street. I had always been considered a decent man. My fellow workers enjoyed my company, my wife worshipped often at our temple and I had paid all the required temple donations. I did not attend the worship services very often, finding them a bit of a bore, but as far as I was concerned, I did enough, I did what was necessary. Now Jesus was inviting me to a faith beyond my understanding and will.

With his simple request to talk to him, probably just to keep his mind occupied by something other than his pain, I began to question whether I could truly commit myself to anyone or anything. I had certainly bound myself in marriage, but family and society expected that. His question at first seemed shallow, until it began to burrow deep into my mind. Suddenly I found myself questioning myself in ways I had not for many years. I wondered how I could continue to skirt life and its responsibilities any longer. Here was the challenge I had avoided with such talent, a challenge to care again, to help carry the crosses of those too weak to shoulder their own. Here was the challenge my cold heart needed to hear if I was to ever be involved in more than my own comfort, if I was ever to truly care about a life other than my own.

My friends, if you could have looked into the face of this Jesus, as I did, you too would know in your hearts that you cannot live in convenient detachment while others go without some basic necessity of life, and still call yourselves followers of the Lord's way. You could not live on the comfortable heights of callous piety, as I did, while your brothers and sisters suffer from injustice. If you could have looked into his eyes, you too would know that this Christ's way demands that you speak out, that you get out of your ivory tower or comfortable distractions to stand face-to-face with the real-life world of people in need.

Have you ever looked into the face of Jesus as he stumbles along next to you in that abused child, in that addict, in that helpless elder, in that lost teen, in that hungry neighbor? If you have looked into the eyes of the homeless person, the Jesus who walks the path of crucifixion through your city streets and have not been transformed, your heart is indeed cold.

Now don't get me wrong. I am not saying that Jesus demands that you take someone else's cross upon your shoulders merely to increase your suffering, as though greater pain would bring you a greater reward. No, Jesus simply challenges you to help others carry what life has burdened them with, for the sake of love. You could help with a strengthening look of encouragement, a confident touch of understanding or a protest against injustice. In what way you help is not as important as the fact that you do help, that you act upon what you say you believe. Standing idly by is not the stance of one who follows Christ's way.

When Jesus asked me to talk to him of my faith, at first I could only respond with fear. I had blessed few in my life, but had cursed many with an aloofness that enabled me to laugh away any involvement. For this coldheartedness I felt ashamed. Now, however, Jesus looks into your eyes and asks you to "talk to me of your faith." How are you going to respond, my friends? Does your faith live in actions, or is it merely dying with protective piety, as mine was; a piety that helps no one carry any burden any way?

Prayer

God, creator of all that is and ever will be, help me draw ever closer to you as I travel along your path each day.

Teach me to take the road less traveled, to share hope instead of despair, build peace rather than conflict, encourage rather than enslave with fear, to give with love and not merely to tolerate. Help me to be involved along the way instead of living indifferently.

Guide me, Lord of life, along the most difficult roads, when pain confronts me, hurt inflicts me, grief haunts me, and sorrow blocks my way. When others are in need of my help, empower me to give beyond measure.

In the face of loneliness, I know that I am never alone, for you, the God of all creation, the almighty source and eternal companion, are there, helping me carry whatever burden is mine.

Divine companion, journey with me today and every day along the crossroads of hope and new beginnings. Amen.

Mary, the Mother

Near the cross of Jesus there stood his mother, his mother's sister, Mary the wife of Clopas, and Mary Magdalene. Seeing his mother there with the disciple whom he loved, Jesus said to his mother, "Woman, there is your son." (*John 19:25-26*)

I don't know where people have gotten the strange ideas that my son "lost" his life. Jesus did not lose his life, he gave it. He died as he lived, with intense love.

Let me also correct the notion that somehow my son wanted to die. He did everything he could to avoid such a fate, save compromising the values and principles he lived so passionately for. Every ounce of his body and heart loved life; he was fully involved with the joys and sorrows of everyday living. He did not want to die, any more than I, his mother, wanted him to face such a cruel fate. My son died because he lived fully, blessing even when it would have been acceptable to curse. He died because he was a threat to those without faith, the hypocrites, bigots, tyrants, money-changers and oppressive scribes and elders possessed by fear.

It was my son's depth of love that challenged the shallow facade of a political structure steeped in greed. When the insecure are threatened with revelation, they often strike out blindly at whatever gets in their way. They are not that different from wounded animals, scared and vicious. I frequently begged Jesus to be sure of what he said and did. Jesus was not a rash or impulsive man (despite his boyhood tendency to run off without a word to Joseph or me as to where he was going). But I felt it necessary during the dangerous last few days of his life to ask him to pray often for the guidance of God, as I prayed for the strength to endure whatever would come.

I was warned, many years ago, by a wise old friend named Simeon that sorrow and pain would pierce my heart, but I never expected that it would lead Jesus to a wooden beam of torment. I would have willingly paid the price for him, if it were possible, but such was not the will of the one who sent my son into the world.

I knew my son's faithful honesty tested the limits of those in authority, but I never imagined that the ultimate demand of love would be required. What mother could believe such a possibility? What deep and agonizing sadness attacked me as I watched my son mocked by the crowds, beaten by the soldiers, and crucified by those who were crazed with fear and anger. Some of Jesus' disciples tried to convince me not to stay with my son during his torment. "What mother can let her child suffer alone?" I responded. With every step he took on the path of his passionate life I was there. I was determined to stay with him until he gave himself to the one who sent him. Although my heart broke with a sorrow so deep I thought I would not endure, I stayed. As I stood beneath my son's cross, I could not help but remember something my husband Joseph often said, "Life is still a blessing, even when you refuse to accept it." The memory helped me stand firmly by my son in his horror and his love. In grief I wailed with tears, in anger I raged with protest, but I remained standing for all to see. As Jesus was crucified, so was I.

From the moment of my deepest agony, standing beneath my son's cross, I was destined to stand with all parents who feel helpless as their children venture forth, praying fervently that their sons and daughters have everything they need for a full and free life. I stand with those mothers and fathers who watch as their children are trapped by the crucifying addictions of this world. I stand with the innocent children of the land who suffer the lack of family care and I stand with those who have lost to death the children they loved. No one can know the pain parents feel as they watch their children risk, discover, make mistakes, hurt, fall and, it is hoped, learn to rise again. Yes, I am the mother of Jesus standing beneath his cross as his brothers and sisters suffer today. Will you accept the courage of God and stand with me, my friend?

In earnest I have prayed to understand fully God's call to me to be the mother of the messiah. Through the joy of helping my son grow strong, and the pain of watching him brought low, I have learned the mysterious ways of God. In every moment of my life, in laughter and misunderstanding, in sorrow and love I have found God's blessed presence. Even as I stood at the foot of my son's cross, sharing his every painful breath, I knew that in and through his death the will of God's love would be done. I knew that, in faith, my son and I could not be defeated. He will rise in love, I am sure, while I promise to remain always hope-filled, resilient, and alive to the reality of a world always blessed by God.

I know that even today, my son, Jesus, dies so that others may be free. Never will I feel such sorrow and pain as when my son died for you who listen to my words. Never will I see such enduring and life-giving love as the love my Jesus has for you.

Jesus, my son, go to your God and to the world with your truth. Be as God called you to be: the light, the truth, the way, living in the hearts of all your brothers and sisters. Be love incarnate, alive and thriving, in a blessed world that does not know how much it is graced. I let you go so that you may be one with all that God loves so much. Die gently, my son, knowing I stand with you. Love strongly, my child, for it is the will of the one who is still sending you into the world.

Prayer

*M*ary, humble, wise, and sorrowful mother, you stood at the foot of your son's cross as he died an inhuman and ungodly death. You stood with courage and wisdom, seeing beyond your pain into the message of your son's life. Open my eyes, Mary, so that I too can see through the midst of my hurt into the possibilities of new meaning and hope.

Your heart, Mary, was pierced with the sword of despair yet you trusted in God's purpose and will. Help me see the presence of God in my life when pain blinds me. Teach me to know in mind and heart that in every moment and experience, God is speaking to me of life's blessings.

Help me accept the death of Jesus, your son, as a sign of God's overwhelming and powerful love for me. And, Mary, most holy, give me the courage to let your son rise up in me as he resurrects forever in your faith. Amen.

The Repentant Thief

But the criminal rebuked the one who blasphemed: "Have you no fear of God, seeing you are under the same sentence? We deserve it, after all. We are only paying the price for what we've done, but this man, Jesus, has done nothing wrong." He then said, "Jesus, re-member me when you enter upon your reign." And Je-sus replied, "I assure you: this day you will be with me in paradise." (*Luke 23:40-43*)

There I was, hanging on a wooden beam, for all to see. The humiliation was almost as painful as the physical torment. The Romans knew how to torture a man in unspeakable ways. I hung there for what seemed like days while men and women looked on with disdain. They laughed at me, mocked my name, and cursed my family. These people loathed me because they knew that I was a thief. They did not know my heart, however. They did not see that I wanted very much to love, that I had dreamed. They never saw my wife and daughter who depended on me for protection and care. Oh God, who would help my family now? Who would work to feed them or even steal to feed them? I may be a thief, that I'll admit, but more disgraceful is the fact that I have let down my wife and daughter. At least my death would prevent me from having to live with that despair. The so-called righteous men of rank never asked me why I became a thief. They did not care. They merely passed judgment on another criminal, another of low birth. The shame I felt was enough to kill me. I did not need their sentence of guilt to feel condemned by a life that had cursed me every step of the way.

As I hung on the cross, desperately trying to pull myself up so that I could take a deep breath, I was overcome with wave upon wave of terrifying fear. Never before had I faced such terror and hopelessness. I had to scream out with the pain, begging someone to forgive me, understand me, help me live or die, help me put an end to my shame.

And there he hung, on a cross next to me, the Jesus every-one had spoken about, the one they called a messiah. He, at least, was not guilty of a crime. All he did was make some promises to the crippled and sick. Yet there he hung, sharing crucifixion. I, at least, had committed a crime for my punishment. He had done nothing to deserve such a death.

As I strained to hear what the man on the cross on the far side of Jesus was saying, I realized that my end was near. Finally there would be an escape. That's all I wanted. I wanted to beg forgiveness for the sins of my life and then die. My mask of security and facade of self-assurance had been torn from me and I was abandoned to my empty fate. Stripped before the eyes of those who despised me, and in the sight of the one they call Lord, I felt totally alone and rejected.

I did not know if it was true what they said of this Jesus, that he had the power to forgive sins and raise the dead. I only saw that standing beneath his cross were men and women who must have loved him deeply. There was a small group of women who clung as much to one another as they did to their love for this man. In the eyes of the women there was profound grief. In the eyes of the men, shocking horror. No one stood with concern at the foot of my cross. He must have been someone extraordinary.

In the chaos of my torment, I desperately needed a savior, a messiah. Perhaps he would listen to me for a moment, perhaps he would forgive. If I could only get his attention. Could it be that the only thing that could possibly be left after everything else has been stripped away—dignity, honor, and health—is faith?

I was determined to speak to Jesus about his rumored promise of eternal life, so I called out to him. I waited a moment while he listened to the other crucified thief and realized that the man was mocking Jesus, taunting him with lies. The words shrieked out of me without control, "Jesus, don't listen to him. He is as terrified as I am but does not know what he is saying." It was then that Jesus turned his head, ever so slowly so as to avoid inflicting more anguish. As Jesus looked into my face, my moment of pain seemed to cease and my blood rushed with a sense of hope. Most of my life I had known only rejection and abandonment, until the moment of my greatest misery, when Jesus reached right into my wounds with a look of forgiveness. In that instant I knew this was the one person to whom I could open my heart. I did not have to steal or beg for his acceptance. How long I had needed such a look of compassion!

I tried to speak to Jesus, to tell him all that was in my heart, but my lips would not move. The muscles in my face seemed to tighten further each time I tried to open my lips. I had to speak to him, to tell him how much shame I felt, yet how much I believed in him. Finally, with tremendous strain, I was able to say only, "Jesus, remember me when you enter your kingdom."

When a man like Jesus dies, there is a special kingdom of remembrance awaiting him. Nothing awaits a man like me, however. Nothing but nothingness. No memorial, no peace, no forgiveness.

Yet Jesus heard my heart's pleading and gave to me the greatest of gifts, an invitation to join him in his peace, his hope, his paradise. He did not care about my crime, but saw deeper into my confessing heart and welcomed me. Never before did I know such a sense of serenity as at that moment. It was then that I knew that neither my life of sin nor my inhuman death could take from me the dignity of being one of God's creatures. Forever I would be accepted and loved in the paradise that belonged to Jesus.

My friend, trust in the love of Christ. In moments of desperate hopelessness, when life seems to have cursed you beyond description, or when others condemn you for your mistakes and sins, let the Lord give you a look into the loveliness of his kingdom. Let the Lord give you a glimpse of the eternal life that stretches out before all those who have faith. When it is impossible, believe. When it is improbable, accept. The Lord of life is beyond understanding, but not beyond forgiveness.

Prayer

Lord of life:

Teach me to trust when I fear I will be hurt again.

Teach me to open my heart after it has been wounded.

Teach me to know that failure is just a word of judgment and does not describe who I am.

Teach me that I can learn from mistakes even when I have cured myself of sin.

Teach me that there are no conditions that your love cannot overcome.

Teach me to live hopefully today and tomorrow, and not remorsefully because of yesterday.

Teach me to love others, even when they are narrow-minded, selfish, and cruel.

Teach me that there is often suffering, and that survival is built on finding meaning in that suffering.

Teach me that the measure of my wisdom is equal to the measure of my bewilderment.

Teach me that it is often necessary to suffer for love.

Teach me to forgive myself when no one else but you will dare.

And teach me, Lord of life, that only when it is dark enough will I be able to see the stars. Amen.

John, the Beloved

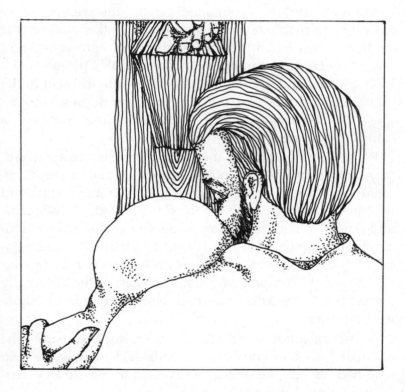

In turn, Jesus said to the disciple whom he loved, "There is your mother." From that hour onward the disciple took Mary into his care. (*John 19:27*)

My name is John. I am a disciple and friend of Jesus. I decided to accept the invitation to speak with you today because of my friendship with the Lord, hoping that you might come to know him as I did.

I understand that my relationship with Jesus had the apparent advantage of his physical presence. But you are not really at a disadvantage just because he died so many years ago. No, faith makes present what is remembered. I know that remembering someone you love is not exactly like the feel of their arm upon your shoulder, but the presence of Jesus is just as real today as it was when I walked, talked and embraced him as brother of my spirit. His presence, right now, may be different, but it is no less real, I promise you. In fact, you could say that Jesus is more fully present in the glory of God today, surrounding you, enveloping you, below you, above you, behind you, and within you. He is standing right next to you.

Remembering enlivens the memory not just in some fantasy, but in some effective and real way. When I say, "I remember Moses, I remember David, I remember Joshua and Abraham," they are with me in all their wisdom, influence, and power. When I say, "I remember Jesus," it is as though my friend stands with me, for in true friendship the relationship never dies. It continues on touching, moving and directing both companions. Just as a shaft of light eternally pierces the darkness, so does friendship forever live in those who experience it.

Do not misunderstand me, however, my friends. On the day that I stood on the Golgotha hillside, watching the man who had opened the secrets of his heart to me die an excruciating death, I did not have such hope and optimism. My tears at that moment tore at my face with a bitterness that almost caused me to run in hiding, as I had done when Jesus was arrested. It was the meaning of our friendship, and what it had done to change me, that kept my feet planted on the earth beneath his cross.

Please do not get the wrong impression. I didn't understand everything my friend told me of his mission or of the God he called Abba. In fact, when we would all recline at night near the fire to talk, Jesus would ramble on with musings that often left me dumbfounded. For a disciple of the Lord, this is not an uncommon position. Friendship, however, does not demand full understanding or even full agreement. Friendship only requires a faith that trusts the other.

I learned over the years to trust my companion, Jesus, enough to drag me to the foot of the cross where he died so violently. Does your confidence in the presence of this friend named savior, messiah, son of God, do the same to you? Does it drive you out of yourself toward those who are crucified today? Does it teach you that yes, life is a tragedy, but it is nonetheless full of joy? Does his blessed friendship for you compel you to return blessing for blessing?

By his love I was transformed. I was made whole. As Jesus hung on the cross in the great gesture of friendship for the world, I promised him that I would not allow him to be forgotten. "Jesus, you will never die," I vowed. "Everyone shall know of your way of eternal hope. I shall tell them. In every corner of the world and every bend of history I shall speak of you. I pledge this as the greatest gift of thanks I can give for what you have given me—friendship. I shall go forth and love as you have taught me, with all that I have, with all that you gave me."

As my heart cried out these words of promise to my brother Jesus, he began to lift his head ever so slightly from its painful resting place, to speak. He looked into the home of my heart, a place that was very familiar to him, and entrusted to me a final gift, a mother. My friend knew, from our late night sharings, of my secret remorse and regret at the loss of my mother when I was too young to understand. So he gave me in his last moments the gift that made me whole. Jesus placed in my care the one person who fully understood him, who loved him like no other could, Mary. "My friend," I said, "I accept the gift of your mother, and thank you for the full kinship of brotherhood. I commit myself to spread, share, plant and nurture this friendship among all those who know their need for something that will truly last forever, a covenant with the God of all."

Friends, you are the Lord's kin if you do what his life commands you to do: love one another as he loved you. Walk in the light of his friendship, lest the darkness overtake you. For I promise that if you walk with him, you will become children of the light that dispels all darkness.

Steps of the Passion

Jesus, sorrowful and lonely in the Garden of Olives, have mercy on the lonely and forgotten of this world.

Jesus, forsaken by your companions, grant us strength when others refuse our friendship.

Jesus, unjustly condemned to death, have mercy on those who suffer from prejudice and hatred.

Jesus, publicly stripped of your garments, have mercy on those who are humiliated and deprived of their human rights.

Jesus, crowned with thorns, mocked and ridiculed, have mercy on those who suffer because of mental anguish.

Jesus, burdened with the weight of the cross, have mercy on us as we struggle and stumble under the weight of life's necessary crosses.

Jesus, suffering on your cross from thirst, have mercy on those who suffer from hunger and want.

Jesus, dying upon your cross, abandoned by your followers, have mercy on those who are dying in loneliness this day.

Jesus, taken down from your cross and laid in the arms of your sorrowing mother, have mercy on those who grieve the loss of loved ones.

Jesus, laid to rest in the dark tomb, have mercy on us, that we might have the courage never to deny in the darkness of pain the light of your resurrection.

Jesus, have mercy, and rise up in me today and every day. Amen.

Conclusion

Lent, and the individuals who have crossed the bounds of time to share themselves in this book, teach me something about the God I do and do not believe in. I do not believe in a God who:

enjoys human suffering
hates the world
refuses people fun
blesses corrupt authority
likes being feared
belongs to only one church or one class of people
can't laugh at foolish human mistakes
casts people into hell for all eternity for the slightest
    infraction of dogmatic rules
can't enjoy a baby crying in church
has been captured by philosophical concepts
is understood by those who refuse to love
is worshipped in church but is forgotten on the streets
believes sex is evil
promises pie only in the sky and not a slice today
provides middle-class comforts
chooses sides in war
gives the answers to life's mysteries only to a select few
demands large donations in exchange for eternal reward
can't transform every person with love

believes human nature is inherently corrupt
hides when men and women are in need
excludes from worship those who struggle with doubts,
    sexuality, or anger at the church
compromises the spirit for the letter of the law
proclaims, "I'll get you some day"
created humanity, but then left us to our own devices
ignores the promise to be with us till the end of time
whose name is not hope
is as small as I am.

Lent, and those men and women who were there at the crucifixion of Jesus and have imaginatively shared themselves in this little book, teach me to believe in God who is:

new life
everything we honestly love
full of surprises
faithful to every promise
eternally young
free to all who choose freely
within every person, regardless of race, faith, or
    economic class
all good
sensitive to those who fail, sin, and make mistakes
weak
the foundation of all
still being crucified today
utterly beyond adequate description
always on the side of truth
laughing at funny human formalities and rituals
always ready to meet us more than halfway
pleased when people simply try
more than our narrow picture of perfection
alive in this world, not just waiting in another

that mysterious "something" that helps us survive the
   loss of loved ones
more than the sum total of human achievement or wishes
beyond all
a personal reality, not just an impersonal force
concerned with justice more than good order
the creator who continues to create today
still teaching those willing to learn
the answer to evil
understanding when habits addict us
suffering in all who suffer
worrisome to those who desire to have power over others
self-revealing through all that is most human
light enough to brighten any darkness
still rising up in hope today.

If the Lord does not rise, love is senseless, and God is absurd. If there is no resurrection, true meaning can never be found in this life. If Jesus did not and does not continue to rise from the futility of the cross and tomb, them life itself becomes unbearable; a mere sham of what it could be. Without the Lord's rising, yesterday and today, the cross teaches only that those who are strongest will survive and those with the most power will control and thrive. Good, purpose, virtue, and courage matter little without resurrection, for only indifference and meaninglessness flow from an empty cross and imprisoning tomb.

Every human heart holds a corner of fear at the possibility that Jesus did not and does not rise, that the Lord is still dying into nothingness. Belief in resurrection is a choice, built only on the promise of Jesus and on a thousand little, everyday experiences of hope. Lent is a time to renew that choice.

Lent is not a season for berating oneself with gloom and self-inflicted shame, morbid grief over personal mistakes or the sins of the world. Nor is it a time for perverse self-hatred for lack of perfect faith.

Lent is a time to wash our faces with hope, to pour the water of service over the feet of those who are crucified today, and to bathe in the daily baptism of new life, which makes us forever one with the risen and rising Christ of Easter.

Of Related Interest. . .

Days of Dust and Ashes
Hope-Filled Lenten Reflections
Pamela Smith SS.C.M.

This day-by-day meditation book reminds readers of their human condition: generally capable, reasonably strong, decent over-all, yet market by vulnerability and certain hesitations and fears. A thread of social justice consciousness is woven throughout the meditations, which end on a note of Easter hope.

ISBN: 0-89622-684-0, 96 pp, $7.95 (order M-84)

40 Days of Grace
Lenten Prayers and Reflections
Laurin J. Wenig

The beauty and power of God's word as reflected in this book continually challenges us to listen to its message in new situations in our lives. Anyone who wants to "walk with the Lord" on his journey to Jerusalem will find much to think about, to pray about and to do, and in the process will accomplish what Ash Wednesday faith demands: a change of heart.

ISBN: 0-89622-665-4, 176 pp, $9.95 (order M-56)

The Parables of Calvary
Reflections on the Seven Last Words of Jesus
Stephen C. Rowan

A unique book! The author compares the last words of Jesus on the Cross with his parables and opens up the rich meanings that affect our lives. A lovely book for all seasons.

ISBN: 0-89622-576-3, 56 pp, $4.95 (order B-77)

Available at religious bookstores or from:

XXIII TWENTY-THIRD PUBLICATIONS
P.O. Box 180 • Mystic, CT 06355
1-800-321-0411
E-Mail:ttpubs@aol.com

QUICK ESCAPES®
PITTSBURGH

"A delightfully well-organized and informative resource for exploring nearby pleasures."

—David Bear, Travel Editor, *Pittsburgh Post-Gazette*

"What a fine idea—a complete seeing/lodging/eating travel guide from your own Pittsburgh-area backyard to sites for weekender trips."

—Al Holliday, Publisher, *Pennsylvania Magazine*

"A wonderful book to peruse for your next quickie trip."

—A. Robert Scott, Publisher, *Pittsburgh Point Magazine*

Help Us Keep This Guide Up to Date

Every effort has been made by the author and editors to make this guide as accurate and useful as possible. However, many things can change after a guide is published—establishments close, phone numbers change, facilities come under new management, etc.

We would love to hear from you concerning your experiences with this guide and how you feel it could be improved and kept up to date. While we may not be able to respond to all comments and suggestions, we'll take them to heart and we'll also make certain to share them with the author. Please send your comments and suggestions to the following address:

The Globe Pequot Press
Reader Response/Editorial Department
P.O. Box 480
Guilford, CT 06437

Or you may e-mail us at:
editorial@globe-pequot.com

Thanks for your input, and happy travels!